Sj

This is me with my camera ...

My Big Cats Journal *Steve Bloom*

... and this is just one of the animals that we'll get to see!

The journey starts here ...

My Big Cats Journal

In search of lions, leopards, cheetahs and tigers

Steve Bloom

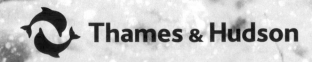

Thames & Hudson

The expedition ...

6–7
Setting off ...

Meet your guide – the photographer Steve Bloom. Discover the route you're going to take and the big cats that you're likely to see.

The adventure starts in Africa in the company of lions.

8–17 ▲
King of the beasts

Days 1 to 10 On the trail of the king of the grasslands, the mighty lion.

◀ 18–27
Leopard watch

Days 11 to 20 Be patient! Wait for the perfect shot of the night hunter, the leopard.

Next, we go leopard spotting.

Still in Africa, we try to keep up with the speedy cheetah.

The journey ends in Asia, in tiger country.

Setting off ...

Hi. I'm Steve Bloom, a wildlife photographer. I took the photos of the lions, leopards, cheetahs and tigers in this book. These animals are known as big cats. Join me on my incredible adventures to capture these magnificent creatures on camera in the wild. Let's get the perfect shot!

Look out for my top tips on using your camera.

AFRICA

▼ Days 1 to 10

My journey starts in Kenya. I travel in a bumpy safari truck across the huge grassland to photograph a family of lions hunting, playing and resting.

Lions

Kenya

Journey starts here

Leopards

Cheetahs

Namibia

A male lion relaxing.

A sneaky peek at a leopard.

Northern China

Journey ends

A Siberian tiger on the prowl.

ASIA

Siberian tigers

Bengal tigers

India

N

Days 31 to 40

I make the long trek to India in search of Bengal tigers, and finally to icy northern China to see the Siberian tiger. Tigers are among the most powerful animals on the planet, but their future is threatened.

A mother cheetah keeps a lookout with her cub.

Days 11 to 20

My next stop is the hot dry bushland further south in Namibia. Here, I catch a glimpse of the most secretive of all the big cats – the leopard.

Days 21 to 30

I stay in Namibia to watch the cheetahs roaming the grassland. Getting a shot of these sleek speed machines can be tricky!

King of the beasts

Day 1 ▷

It's hot and dusty here on the African grassland. When I look out of the safari truck, I immediately see a lion! With its strong body and powerful paws, you know this big cat is in charge. Its only enemies are humans and other lions. I drive as close as I can and take my first picture.

LION IN CLOSE-UP

Name:	*the scientific name for lion is 'Panthera leo'*
Found:	*in parts of Africa and a small area in India, Asia*
Habitat:	*grassland and dry scrubland*
Favourite food:	*buffalo, zebra, warthog*
Lives for:	*about 14 years*
Number of young:	*up to four at a time*

A male lion keeps a watchful eye out for intruders.

8

On the way to the waterhole in the cool of the morning.

Family time

Days 2 to 4 ▽

After several days, I finally get the photograph I've been waiting for! Lions are the only big cats that usually live in groups. A group is called a pride, and can often include up to 20 females with their cubs, as well as a few males. Here, some pride members are walking over a hill towards a waterhole for a drink.

Young cubs

I'm lucky to see a lioness with young cubs. When the cubs are newly born, she keeps them safe in a den away from the rest of the pride. At first they are blind, but after about ten days they open their eyes. After six weeks, they step outside. It's still a private time though, so I take great care not to disturb the new family.

The lion cubs search for a nourishing drink of milk.

◀ Day 5

For the first few months of their lives, the cubs feed mainly on their mother's milk, drinking it through the teats on her belly. Later, they start to eat the meat she brings back for them as well.

A lioness carries her cub by the loose skin on the back of its neck.

Day 6 ▶

From time to time, a lioness carries her young to a new den, especially if she senses danger from leopards and hyenas, which might attack them. Even though her teeth are razor-sharp, she can pick cubs up so delicately they hardly feel a thing. A new den will have no scent, making it harder for enemies to find.

A lion's tongue is rough like sandpaper to 'comb' out any loose hairs.

▲ Day 7

As the cubs get bigger, they become more adventurous and start to explore. But they still stay close to their mother for protection. She will look after them for up to 18 months. Here the cubs are getting a good lick clean!

Growing up

Life is tough for young lion cubs. Very few of them will survive and grow up into adults. I watch this pride for a couple of days and see that the lionesses also look after cubs that aren't their own. This extra help can make all the difference to a cub's chance of survival. The pride is like a big family with lots of cousins.

One day, this play-fighting will be for real.

▲ Day 8

The young lion cubs spend a lot of their time play-fighting. This is a way of learning how to hunt and deciding who is 'top cat'. It gives them a better chance of making it to adulthood.

A young male lion sets off for his new life away from the pride.

Hunting ▽

As a male lion grows up, he develops a big shaggy mane. It makes him look fierce and strong. Male lions are the only big cats to have manes.

▲ Day 9

The pride is uncomfortable that this young male is still around. He senses that it's time to leave. This usually happens to a male aged between two and four years.

Sleeping ▽

Lions sleep for over 20 hours a day. If you want to photograph them in action, that means a lot of waiting around!

Top Tips

Take photos through an open window, resting the camera on a beanbag to keep it steady. When on safari, ask the guide if it is safe to do so.

On a lion hunt

It's terrifying watching lions hunt! Usually the lionesses catch dinner for the pride, working in teams. Many of the animals they chase, such as gazelles, buffalo and zebras, can run faster than they do, so the cats have developed clever ways to surprise them.

A lioness drags a buffalo to the ground with her powerful paws.

Day 10 ▽

On my last day here, the lions are hungry. At dusk I watch them in action. Early morning is also a common time for them to hunt.

TOP HUNTING TACTICS

1. Stalk ▷ and observe

A lioness creeps up on a group of zebras. She keeps her body low to the ground so that she can sneak through the grass without being spotted. Then she sits and waits patiently.

The zebras graze, unaware of the lion's presence.

In a panic, the zebras sprint off in all directions.

◁ ## 2. Pounce and surprise

When the moment is right, she pounces. This sends the zebras into a complete panic and they begin to run wildly. The lioness has caught the zebras off guard, so she has the advantage.

3. Chase ▷ and trap

The lioness singles out one zebra and gives chase. To help her, other lions may circle the zebra at a distance. Eventually the animal will be trapped on all sides.

The lioness is about to catch the zebra!

Leopard watch

Day 11 ▷

I pack my bags and head off in search of leopards. These creatures are the most common big cats in Africa but the hardest of all to find. By day, they often hide in the trees, then at night creep down to hunt for food. They usually live alone. I am prepared for a long wait in the dark.

LEOPARD IN CLOSE-UP

Name:	*the scientific name for leopard is "Panthera pardus"*
Found:	*in much of Africa and parts of Asia*
Habitat:	*woodland, grassland and river forests*
Favorite food:	*everything from monkeys to insects*
Lives for:	*about twelve years*
Number of young:	*between two and four cubs*

When darkness falls, my patience pays off – a male leopard peers down from a branch!

Amazing senses
Days 12 to 16

Night after night I watch the leopards, amazed by
their powerful senses and lightning-quick reactions.
They use their senses to track down food and to stay
alert in case other animals try to steal their kills.

Hearing ▷

A leopard has excellent hearing. It can
swivel its ears forwards and backwards to
find the direction of sounds. It can hear
noises that our ears can't even pick up.

This leopard turns its head towards a nearby sound.

A leopard can 'smell' with its mouth open.

◁ Smelling

A leopard has a much better sense
of smell than humans. This allows
it to find food quickly and sense
whether other animals have been
in its territory. Strangely, it has a
smell gland just above its mouth
that lets it 'taste' smells.

Seeing ▷

Night sight is another leopard super-sense. A leopard can usually see better in the dark than the animals it hunts to eat. This gives it a huge advantage. A leopard also has a special layer at the back of its eyes that directs extra light farther back, allowing it to see as much as possible at night.

In the dark, a leopard's eye lets in more light to see better.

Sensitive whiskers help to detect close objects.

◁ Touching

Long thick whiskers grow on either side of a cat's mouth. As it moves through the undergrowth, the whiskers help it to feel objects near by. This way the cat builds up a 'touchy-feely' picture of its surroundings.

Top Tips

Work like a detective! Follow tracks such as paw prints that will tell you an animal has been near by. Look for an outline in a tree.

21

Superb spots

This female leopard shows off her magnificent spotted fur coat!

 # Day 17

Today, I see a leopard prowling around at dusk. Here you can see its spotted fur coat clearly, but when this leopard is up in the trees it will be hidden. The dark spots break up its outline and help it to blend in with the leaves. It's the perfect camouflage.

Spot the difference

Can you tell the difference between these two sets of spots? Which big cats do you think they belong to?

A

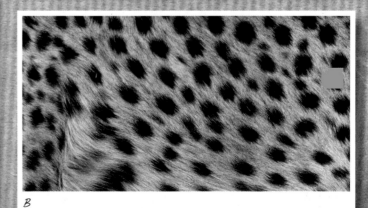

B

Answer

A. These are a leopard's spots. They have a blotchy shape and are called rosettes.
B. These are a cheetah's spots. Each one is solid.

On the attack

Leopards are one of the smallest big cats, but they can easily kill animals twice their size. Seeing them attack shows me just how dangerous they are. Leopards aren't fussy about what they hunt and this has helped them to survive well in the wild.

Powerful muscles ripple through this leopard's body as it hunts.

▲Day 18

It's almost sunset and I spot this leopard stalking an antelope. Tomorrow, it may hunt a young giraffe, a monkey or even feast on some insects. I steady my camera and press the shutter.

FEAST IN A TREE

Before a leopard eats its dinner it takes it back up into a tree. It drags its food up the trunk, gripping it by the neck with its sharp teeth, then it drapes it over a branch.

Here it can eat safely, out of the reach of other animals. It may even save some leftovers for later.

As a leopard goes in for the kill, its claws come out.

◭ Day 19

Here's a leopard about to pounce! It uses its front legs to grab its prey and digs in its sharp claws for a tight grip. Then it gives a swift bite to the back of the neck or the throat. It usually takes just one deadly bite to finish off the victim.

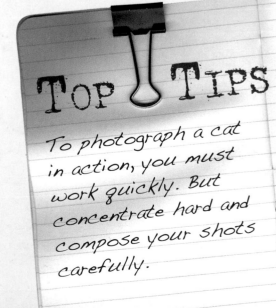

Top Tips

To photograph a cat in action, you must work quickly. But concentrate hard and compose your shots carefully.

Types of leopard

Around the world, there are several types of leopard. They look different from the ones I am photographing here in Africa because they have adapted to suit the surroundings where they live.

An African leopard creeps down from a thorny Acacia tree.

▲ Day 20

I took this shot as the sun went down. African leopards have straw-yellow coats that blend in with the hot dusty scrubland and river forests. Their fur is short and sleek to suit the hot weather. They are the type of leopard most people know.

Around the world

Here are some photos from my other travels. Snow leopards and black panthers are mostly found in Asia. Both are extremely rare sights.

Black panther ▷

A black panther makes its home in tropical rainforests where it is almost invisible. It has black spots like an African leopard but you cannot see them easily against its dark fur.

▽ Snow leopard

Snow leopards live high up in cold mountains. They have longer fur than other leopards to keep them warm. They even have fur between the pads on their feet. During winter, their spotted silvery coats help them to blend in with the rocks and snow.

Close up, the panther's black fur looks almost like silk.

A snow leopard with its two young cubs.

The cheetah chase

A cheetah can reach the speed of a car on a motorway in under three seconds!

In daylight, I head back to the open grassland to find the smallest and lightest of the big cats – the cheetah. Its slim body and thin, powerful legs make it one incredible speed machine. A female sprints by. I keep her eye in the same part of the frame while I follow her with the camera. Then I press the shutter, catching her in action while blurring the background.

CHEETAH IN CLOSE-UP

Name:	comes from the Hindi word meaning 'spotted one'
Found:	in parts of Africa and a small area in Asia
Habitat:	grassland, scrubland and some mountain areas
Favourite food:	gazelle, impala, young zebras
Lives for:	about 12 years
Number of young:	up to five at a time

Raising young

Watching a female cheetah with her cubs is fascinating.
She usually has between three and five at a time. For the first
two years, she teaches them the skills they need to survive.
Then she leaves them alone in the wild. It's a tough life.

The cubs' spotty fur helps to hide them in the grass and rocks.

▼ Days 22 to 25

For several days, I have been tracking this cheetah family, learning about how they hunt, care for each other and feed themselves.

A Day in the Life of a Cheetah

06:00 ▷
The cheetah mother leaves her cubs hidden in the long grass and goes off hunting.

07:00
After an hour of careful stalking, she breaks into a sprint and catches a gazelle. Then she rests.

The mother cheetah on the hunt.

A vulture spots a snack.

▲ **07:30**
The cheetah calls her cubs over to enjoy the meat breakfast. The vultures circle, waiting for them to finish so that they can pick over the bones.

12:00 to 16:00
It is the hottest part of the day. The cheetah and her cubs sleep in the long grass.

16:30 ▷
The mother is worried. What can she hear? She moves her cubs regularly to keep them safe from predators such as lions.

The cubs are growing up quickly.

The chase

Day 26

The chase is on and I need to think fast otherwise I'll miss the action! Unlike most big cats, a cheetah hunts in the daytime. It moves so quickly that the chase and kill can be over in less than one minute.

A cheetah springs into action.

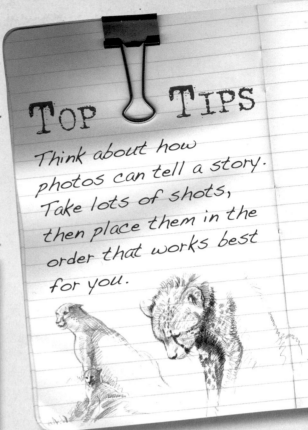

◀ Get set, go

This cheetah has seen a gazelle. When the gazelle is close by, the cheetah bounds out of the bushes. Although the cheetah can run fast, it cannot keep up the pace for long without getting tired.

On the move ▶

When a cheetah runs, it takes huge strides using the powerful muscles in its long legs. As it leaps forwards, it stretches out its whole body and lifts all four feet off the ground. A cheetah cannot pull in its claws like other cats. When it lands, the claws give a firm grip, like the spikes on running shoes.

1. The cheetah pushes off on its back legs.

32

Look at the concentration on the animal's face as it runs.

▲ Full sprint ahead

A cheetah can run, leap and turn at high speed using its long tail
to keep balance. The type of cheetah in this picture is called a king
cheetah. It has black stripes running along its back instead of spots.

2. It bounds forwards and stretches out.

3. It draws its legs together to leap again.

Deadly design

A cheetah's streamlined body makes it an excellent hunter. But here on the African plains, there is danger from more powerful lions and leopards, so a cheetah needs to protect itself too.

Days 27 to 30

Over my last days, I see how the cheetahs use their skills to survive in the wild.

▼ Hackles up

This young male feels threatened when he spots another animal. He tries to make himself look bigger and more fierce by showing his teeth and raising the fur on the back of his neck.

A cheetah is the world's fastest land animal.

Spiky fur and a snarl make this young animal look terrifying.

▲ Long legs

At full sprint, a cheetah can take almost three strides a second on its long legs! This not only helps it to catch dinner easily but also lets it escape from animals that are more powerful but not so fast.

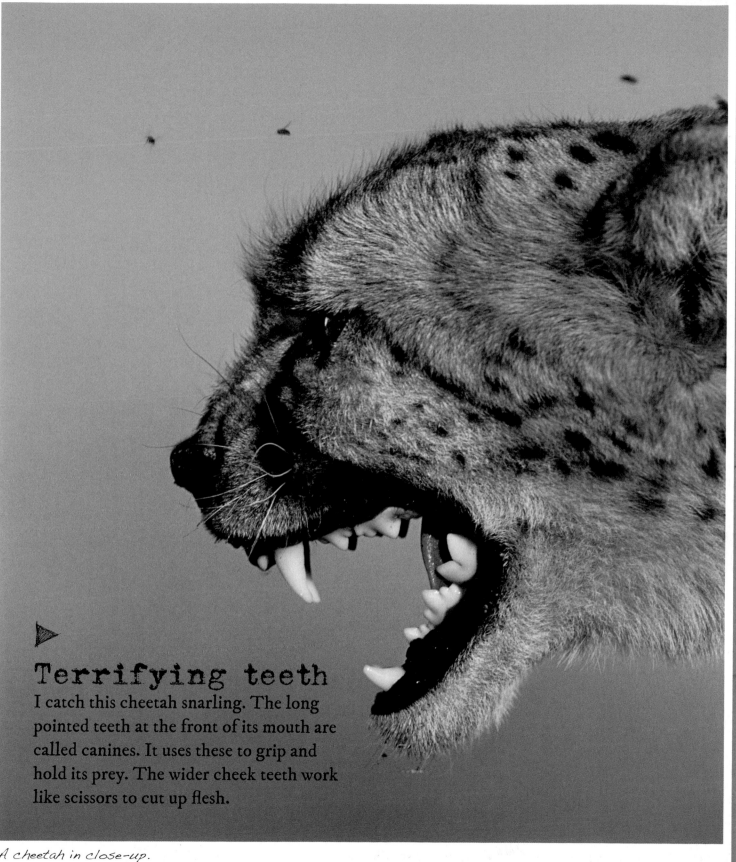

Terrifying teeth

I catch this cheetah snarling. The long pointed teeth at the front of its mouth are called canines. It uses these to grip and hold its prey. The wider cheek teeth work like scissors to cut up flesh.

A cheetah in close-up.

Tiger trail

Day 31 ▷

My journey now takes me to a vast wildlife park in India, southern Asia. It is one of the few places left in the world where you can find the biggest and most powerful cat of all – the tiger. This magnificent hunter is extremely rare and it is protected here. I am lucky to see one so close by and take my first picture.

TIGER IN CLOSE-UP

Name:	the scientific name for tiger is 'Panthera tigris'
Found:	in parts of Asia
Habitat:	mountains, river forests, rainforests
Favourite food:	wild boar, deer, moose, buffalo
Lives for:	about 15 years
Number of young:	between two and four at a time

Here you can clearly see the tiger's beautiful markings. This photo was taken

from way up on an elephant's back!

Types of tiger

There are two well-known types of tiger – the Bengal tiger and the Siberian tiger. They live in different places but look similar. Take a close look at my photos and see if you can spot any differences between them.

A Bengal tiger relaxes in the shade of the trees.

▲ Bengal tiger

I find this magnificent big cat cooling off near a stream. Bengal tigers make their homes in warm forests and have short fur with rich brown stripes. An adult male can weigh as much as 200 kg.

Day 32 ▷

Photographing a Bengal tiger is tricky. They go to places where cars cannot drive and it's too dangerous to look for them on foot. The best way to see them is from the back of an elephant. I have to climb up a ladder to get to the seat on the top!

When you ride on an elephant, you bounce all over the place! Make sure you hold your camera tightly.

◁ Siberian tiger

The Siberian tiger is also called the Amur tiger. It lives in cold mountain forests. It has longer fur than the Bengal tiger and a thick layer of fat on its belly to keep it warm. Siberian tigers usually grow larger than Bengal tigers. They can weigh up to 300 kg – that's about the same as three adult men!

Thick fur keeps the Siberian tiger warm in its icy home.

Hunting ground

My final stop is icy northern China to watch the Siberian tigers prowling around their territory. Tigers usually live alone and cover huge areas of the forest looking for food. They have enormous appetites, eating up to 27 kg of meat in a single night. That's about 240 hamburgers in one go!

Feeling comfortable, this tiger licks its fur clean with its tongue.

▲ Day 33

I come across this relaxed young male – though his mood may change if another tiger enters his area. Tigers often have vicious fights and may even kill one another in battle.

Despite its huge size, a tiger can run swiftly and gracefully.

▲ Day 34

A tiger chases its dinner. Normally, it waits patiently behind a tree, then leaps out when an animal passes by. Siberian tigers feed on wild boar, moose and deer. When they're full, they may cover the body with snow and return to finish off the leftovers later.

TOP TIPS

In cold weather, a camera's charge drains quickly. Keep the camera warm inside your clothing, together with a spare battery.

Sharp claws

Have you ever watched a pet cat sharpen its claws on a post? Tigers do the same but they use a tree trunk. This keeps their claws in perfect condition for hunting.

In the water

Unusually for cats, tigers enjoy being in the water. They are strong swimmers and may even chase their prey into rivers.

41

Tigers in danger

Days 35-40

It's sad, but there are only a few thousand tigers left on our planet. This mighty animal might disappear for good. Photographing the Siberian tigers here seems more important than ever.

Hunted ▽

In the past, tigers were hunted for their beautiful fur and their body parts, which were used in medicines. Today hunting is banned but it still happens.

Very few tigers now live truly in the wild.

△In peril

Humans are the biggest threat to tigers. Over the years, they have chopped down trees to clear the land for farming. This has taken away the tigers' forest home and the animals they need to eat to survive.

Tigers may look fierce but they are under threat from humans.

Project Tiger

In 1972, in India, a project was set up to save the Bengal tiger. Since it started, over 40 wildlife parks have been opened where the animals can roam safely. Life is still tough though for the Bengal tiger and numbers are falling.

A protected Bengal tiger.

Two Siberian tigers get to know each other.

▲ The future

Here, in icy northern China, scientists are working hard to save the Siberian tiger through special breeding programmes. Let's hope that one day this friendly pair I snapped will produce their own little cubs.

Steve's photo tips

Taking photos of animals is brilliant fun and you don't
have to go on a safari to do it. You could photograph
a pet in the back garden, snap birds and insects in
the park or take your camera on a day out to the zoo.
Check out my tips and get started!

▶ 1. Frame your shot

It's a good idea to think about how all
the parts of your picture fit together.
This is called framing. Decide on the
most important thing and place it in the
viewfinder. Then look at the rest of the
picture. Is it well balanced? What is at
the edges?

Here, a mother cheetah and her cute cub are framed by the
long blades of grass.

I took advantage of the setting sun to create
this evening shot.

◀ 2. Use the light

When you take pictures outside, you
are working with natural light. Don't
worry about clouds, as these will give
your photos a softer look, but do avoid
shooting into direct sunlight. If the flash
is on low power and used in the daytime,
it can lighten dark shadows and give a
sparkle to the eyes. Use it wisely though,
and be careful not to startle the animals.

When the mother lion licked her cub, I was ready to click!

MORE TOP TIPS

* Always behave calmly around animals. If you make a fuss, they'll probably run off.

* When you are with animals, don't spend too much time looking at your pictures. You can do that at home.

* Experiment with different angles and develop your own style. Look in photography books for ideas.

▲ 3. Catch a moment

Unlike people and a few obedient pets, wild animals rarely sit still when you want them to! Catching the perfect moment takes patience and luck. One tip is to watch the animals and get to know their behaviour. This can help you to guess what they might do next.

At eye level it feels like this tiger is looking at us!

◄ 4. Go in close

This is your chance to capture an animal's personality. Get as close as you can to your subject without disturbing it, then focus in on the eyes to take the shot. If you take a picture at the same eye level as the animal, it will make it feel really personal.

Photo projects

The best way to develop your photography skills is by practising. It took me many years to learn about photography. You must try hard and be patient. At home, think about which pictures you like and why. Build up a photo scrapbook using my project ideas below.

▷ Animal action

Animals are often on the move. They may run, jump, swim or fly. Have a go at photographing different animals in action and create a poster or collage on the computer. You could take pictures of dogs, squirrels, ducks, pigeons or butterflies.

Fast as lightning!

Photo diary

Photograph your pet, showing all the different things it does over one day. Choose the best pictures and put them in order with captions to make your pet its very own photo diary.

9:00
Bingo enjoys a tasty breakfast.

13:00
Whoops! He's stuck in a tree.

20:00
What an adventure. Time to snooze.

A funny story

Have you ever thought about how photos can tell a story? They can really bring a tale to life. Here's a funny thing that happened to me on safari in Africa ...

 2 – I was in a safari truck with no windows. I sat there terrified as the lion came too close for comfort.

 1 – One day, a very large lion with a beautiful mane walked up to me.

 3 – Guess what? The lion let out a giant burp! It smelt of the worst rotten eggs you could imagine. Then before I knew it, he walked off!

Now tell me your own photo story!

Index

For my son Dan

First published in the United Kingdom in 2012 by
Thames & Hudson Ltd, 181A High Holborn,
London WC1V 7QX

Photographs copyright © 2012 Steve Bloom
www.stevebloom.com
Text copyright © 2012 Thames & Hudson Ltd, London
Illustrations copyright © 2012 Thames & Hudson Ltd, London
Illustrations by David Bezzina
Researched and edited by Deborah Kespert
Consultant Barbara Taylor

British Library Cataloguing-in-Publication Data
A catalogue record for this book is available from the
British Library
ISBN 978-0-500-65002-8

Printed and bound in Singapore by Imago

To find out about all our publications, please visit
www.thamesandhudson.com. There you can subscribe
to our e-newsletter, browse or download our current
catalogue, and buy any titles that are in print.

SIZE AND SPEED

cheetah	leopard	lion	tiger
weight	**weight**	**weight**	**weight**
up to 65 kg	up to 70 kg	up to 250 kg	up to 300 kg
speed	**speed**	**speed**	**speed**
up to 113 km per hour	up to 60 km per hour	up to 80 km per hour	up to 90 km per ho